I0182544

About A Girl

Fareh Iqbal

Copyright © 2016 Fareh Iqbal
All rights reserved.
ISBN 13: 978-1775076117
ISBN-10: 17750776113

For beating hearts and open minds.

Lend thy pen, dear Spirit
and guide me well
my words fall short and broken,
while thine in beloved scripture
continue to dwell.

Surrender thy ink, dear Spirit
and allow it to stain,
with verses that imprint
themselves into hearts
and echo within chambers of the brain.

Offer thy parchment, dear Spirit
that I too may inspire
the pens and hearts
of the many that will come after me
long after my soul escapes
and mortal dwelling expires.

Paper Doll

Born the lovechild of paper and ink,
trace my roots to the beginning
when all was one
yet incomplete.
When a thought
sprang forth life
and the touch of ink,
a soul.
An artist's muse
entwined with poetic desire,
'ere I exist.
The fragments of my being scatter in Time
ribbons of memory stray in thy ocean,
as your fingertips send shivers
down the creases in my cracked spine.
Forever enclosed in letters
we begin to sink,
and when you touch me gentle Reader,
I bleed ink.

Her words fell
black ink on white lines
breaking,
struggling and straining
to rhyme.

Her thoughts collected dust,
decay and rust
in the restless solitude
of her mind.

If the stars fail to align on earthly plains

and celestial beings in the heavens are at war,

when humanity is out of tune,

a fractured refrain,

is Love glory worth dying for?

Tears fell across her pillow
burning like midnight diamonds
that fractured her heart
into broken constellations.

He came to her
in traces of moonlight and shadow
repairing her shattered sky
with every beautiful word spoken.

To be consumed,

consumed whole.

To be destroyed,

destroyed utterly.

To be left,

completely bereft.

To die,

a thousand and one nights,

and to return at dawn

irrevocably,

inevitably,

insatiably,

for more.

All I want

are your hands,

old,

soft,

wrinkled

with Time,

cracked

with age,

forever entwined

in mine.

His touch

calmed

the shattered tempo

of her melancholy heart,

and she found it easier

to exhale

once more.

Her words

provoked

the hazy tranquility

of his apathy,

and he found himself

struggling to recapture

remnants of lost serenity.

He,

with eyes so clear and steadfast,

twin reservoirs of endless patience

tamed the wilderness

etched beneath her skin

and soothed her reckless inclinations.

He became poetry

as she outlined him lovingly with prose,

his features lined with words

that could not betray her page with woes.

Safely bound in paper and ink

was how he remained constant always,

as she filled the blank spaces of their history

lost in the enchantment of someday.

Before you

What was once precious,

pales in tones

of insignificance.

What was once everything,

fades to the background

all that manifests is your presence.

Now I understand,

upon Earth's battlegrounds

there can exist slivers of heaven.

Greed

Your touch
will never imprint my skin
long enough.
Your taste
will never quench my thirst
deep enough.
Your presence
will never ease my longing
quite enough.
Nothing
will ever satisfy
my greed for you.

Entwined

To entwine thy heart and soul
and every nuance of thy mind,
to feed off thy words
and lose all sense of sensibility and time.

To immerse into every inflection of thy voice
and come up savouring each syllable,
to wrap in the warm cocoon of thy embrace
secure in a love rendered inevitable.

Starry Night

Far better
than sleep and dreams
is to lie awake
and rename constellations
burning through the starry night
in your arms.

Love is

the redemption

of thy touch.

Home is

the steady beat

of thy heart.

Enchantment is

the summer afternoons

in thy arms.

And forever

is a destination

beside thee.

Patience

Had I known
it was to be you,
sweet patience would have tempered
my every restless inclination,
my every tempestuous move.

I would have waited
counting stars and sunsets,
rather than remain
a slave bound to my foolish regret.

One

With every inflection of gold

his eyes claimed her.

Bewitched,

bewildered,

she slipped further

under his spell

so effortlessly woven

leaving no room for doubts

or promises unspoken.

Her heart burst into a thousand fragments

glistening like morning dew in the rising sun.

Unraveled,

unwoven,

she fell prey

to the beauty

of his endless torment.

Traces

I wonder

if you can read the words

etched on my skin

like invisible tattoos

where poetry and prose

mingle with flesh

that yearn to absorb

all fragments

and whispered traces

of you.

Klopstock

I long for shade under a weeping willow,
the whispering sigh of a gentle breeze,
the sky my blanket,
the earth my pillow
among the flutter of rusty leaves.

Under her shade
verses of the Romantics
will seduce us into untroubled sleep
Byron, Percy, Shelley and Keats.

And when twilight falls
turning the sky to pink rust,
in my heart's secret chamber
amid the fallen leaves in November,
shall lie a perfect picture of us.

Laced Mandolin

Mandolin, Mandolin
laced with paper dreams
and shredded hearts
frayed at the seams.
You sing of whisky nights
empty fights,
and the long hours in between.
Lost in a lullaby
of yesterday's blues,
the years slip by
in a ballad of forgotten youth.

She wished she could capture

the flicker in his eyes

and the taste of his skin

for people are

transitory,

ephemeral,

and to hold him forever

was simply naive

wish fulfillment.

Thy imperfection is perfect
thy fragile presence divine,
memories no longer
torment disbelievers
for in sacred thoughts
you are eternally mine.

If words are wind

you are a hurricane

shredding my peace

into tatters on the floor,

it is no longer a choice

for when thy heart beckons

mine must in kind

follow.

Memories of thee
seduce my discipline
like a siren song.

The imprint of thy taste
stains these parched lips
in an eternal kiss.

The imprint of thy touch
seeps through skin and bone
caressing the depths
of my very soul.

Watching the rain streak tears

against the window pane

into empty hours

of faded summer nights,

memories of you

between every breath

where each moment

is a moment

to get through,

sweet Death

would be a welcome reprieve,

for remembrance of you

will surely be the end of me.

The Aftermath

I look within
trembling to find
broken poems
and empty rhymes.

Dusk and dawn
hold no meaning
the days pass by
with no luxury of dreaming.

Awake in moonlight
burnt out much too soon
seeking out my mind's serenity
in dark and empty rooms.

My resolve to seek temperance
withers and bends
like dusty leaves
drifting in the dry summer wind.

Tangled

There is salvation
in the Poets' written word,
their beloveds immortalized
forever in rhyming verse.

Nostalgia seeps through a painting
tattered from years gone by
capturing the beauty of a moment
in a portrait fraught with human life.

This is the aftermath
where memories entwine
as we lie awake in a stupor
drunk on their fine, aged wine.

Words fail us now for all that is left
are broken thoughts
straining to repair
irrevocably tangled affairs of the heart.

This useless endeavor

your careless silence

the uncertainty of your mind

nurtures my contempt,

precariously treading on the fine line

between love and hate

manifested solely

by your cold indifference.

Dusty Crossroads

There's a need to break free
untangle this mess,
through words and music
her soul begins to undress.
She wants something new
but is left with shades of old,
burdened thoughts and faded dreams
nights so hot they burn cold.
Her tears have bled dry,
stained on her cheeks
they leave a testament
gone is the innocence of a child
who in the wake of heartache
has become a reluctant woman.
In chambers of loneliness
in the trapdoors of her mind
memory haunts like a specter,
the past, dear Reader,
is never truly left behind.

She thought she knew where to turn,

where the road ought to have led,

there is nothing where the path once was

save broken crossroads cloaked in 3 a.m. darkness.

Where did she go wrong,

she never meant to go astray

the eternal night begins to close in

while the last light of the world fades away.

Summer Rain

The sun cast its shadow
as we lay there by your window
with the broken glass.
Stretched like cats,
a kaleidoscope of colours floated by
teasing us with easy flight.
Sweet breezes lingered
moist,
with the promise of rain.
The scent of grass tickled our senses,
as your fingers
grazed my legs.
Entwined like lovers,
the days flowed in innocent deliberation
until Dusk crawled in.
The lullaby of our youth
faded away like a floating dream.
In a patch of sunlight
our laughter dwells,
as the clouds swallow the sun.

Day Three

Cease.

Refrain thy footsteps from entering the threshold of dreams.

Let alone what you do not understand.

Do not beckon for reality to intervene

for when it does

shadows writhe in pain.

Allow me to indulge

whilst my demons peacefully slumber,

permit me to enjoy silence

until their cries commence once more.

Turn away,

as I strip my soul,

the horrors of existence

revealed with each shedding of skin.

Tainted with Revelation's dark truth

we are bound you and I

for a future ablaze with cries pleading mercy.

Brace thyself,

as we go up in smoke.

She brings the music

but he is

deaf

to her melody

and his heart

blind

to her aid

preferring to remain

an impervious audience

to her saviour's serenade.

Prisoner

Is loneliness not too a disease
where we wither away
under lock and key
trapped within iron walls
in castles of our own making.

Are we not prisoners
enslaved to false hope
and bound to the promise
of better days to come.

When will we
break the mental shackles
and refuse to remain at the mercy
of false princes
and learn to save ourselves.

I do not know

how to pick up the pieces

you scattered

carelessly

when your fingerprints

stain

every

single

one.

Clouds

Have I lost you
in the long hours of the afternoon
when you disappear
behind isolated clouds of smoke.

Inch by inch,
it creeps over
taking you
away from me.

Your resolve
wilts like a fractured rose
scattering like ash
at the slightest touch.

I beseech my eyes
not to seek thee out,
for it is far too easy
to fall into their trap.

The slope is slippery
and to escape is futile
from the wastelands
of their hazardous depths.

She censored her thoughts
until one by one
they settled into dust.

He couldn't tell why
her conversation had run dry
and her tongue turned to rust.

He was the dream
she had longed for
in all her waking moments.

Once he was realized
and her curiosity satiated,
she much preferred the
slumber of her ignorance.

You say the spark fizzled

'twas your fingers

that extinguished the flame,

shattered at your inability

to temper your words

with consistency,

burning embers lie at my feet,

all of you that remains.

No

Do not

indulge your wandering feet

to lead back to me.

Time

and time.

and time again.

Is this the strains of love unrequited

or the prolonging anguish

of our inevitable end.

Forty Six

It seemed the world had shifted
from its rusted axis,
and the sunrise
held more promise
than remorse.

For now
Time was her ally
and forty six days
meant more
than ten years ever could.

Repentance

I beg forgiveness

for sins unknown,

those forgotten in the past

and those

yet to come.

For my tongue

nor my pen

cannot do justice

to the beatings of my heart,

and my self-preservation

always seems to come

at an irrevocable human cost.

Your heart is an island

in a body of tumultuous tides,

for you are unable to recognize

the oasis of sweet salvation,

basking in your preference

to lay shipwrecked

on broken shores of your own destruction.

You say you have an affliction
that resets your mind's condition,
caught up in the need for constant stimulation
in a habit you never seem to question.

I wish you didn't lack the recognition
to name the truth of your addiction,
you tell me this is your personal revolution
that brings you to the peak of mental ascension.

Through the broken lens of your perception
you feel entitled to this damaged solution,
fatally confusing elixir and poison.

All I can do is watch helplessly
while you are forever bound
to the enslavement of your final retribution.

Her hungry heart
feasted upon his lies,
swallowing every syllable
savouring every bite.

She feasted to quench
the insatiable hunger within,
her heart demanded more
a soothing balm
for this most unhappy condition.

His words stuck in her throat
until she could no longer breathe,
choking on his twisted truth
until her heart had satisfied its greed.

Oatmeal

I allowed myself to think of you today.
And for the first time
it didn't sting.
It didn't end in tears
and recriminations.
Nor bouts of melancholy
or stormy aggravations.
It felt like nothing.

It felt like oatmeal.

Frost

She felt his interest slip away
like an icicle
in the summer sun
slowly
daily
it was barely noticeable
until all traces of his affection
melted
like frost
into the ground.

Unrequited

Perhaps it was best

for us to long for one another

in secret and silence

in the fragile beauty of an unrequited dream

for the aligning of the stars is treacherous

and cruel

and mocking

because you, my darling,

are not at all

what you made yourself seem.

Entrapment

Prisoner

to the whims of your affections.

Torn

between the swinging pendulum

of your mood.

Lost

across the hazy thoughts

that entreat your waking moments.

Helpless

against the broken constellations

that fracture the darkness.

Waiting

until memory returns you to me once more.

Thoughts of you shift

with the tumultuous tide.

Some nights

I surrender to memory.

Some nights

I let the thoughts linger

and wash over me

in waves unsatisfied.

The words burn

on the tip of her tongue

and fall to ashes

while he sleeps.

In the velvet shroud of darkness

blissfully unaware

of what he has begun

unbeknownst to him

her heart silently weeps.

To thee
I am an afterthought,
a passing fancy
a temporary distraction,
mused briefly
then swiftly gone.

To me
you are a bittersweet memory
perfuming my thoughts,
thy fragrance
lingering on.

There is thunder,

raging chaos

inside your mortal shell.

Lightning flows,

electric blue

through the crossroads of your veins.

Jagged flashes,

burn bright

behind the depths of your eyes.

And yet

you remain steadfast,

ever the calm

before the storm.

Thy name is beautiful irony

for like Ahab,

you do not believe.

Unable to break through

the burden of your familial history

collapsing against the thin walls

of your hollow beliefs.

Afterthought

Hours drag
across the wooden floor

how easy for you to forget
that a heart beats for you inside this room

pride forbids me to chastise
yet forces me to contend with the ugly truth

I never thought you to be careless
with the heart of the girl you rescued.

The Illusionist

He promised her
the constellations in the sky
the turquoise rays of a Neptune moon
the celestial beings invisible to her eyes
and forgotten treasure buried deep
in a silver lagoon.

He promised her all that was in the heavens,
starry eyed she believed every syllable
with such devotion
that made holy men pale.

Nothing was in his power to give
except the thrill of smoke and mirrors
and the beauty of illusion.

Phoenix

Love can only rise

from the destruction of pride

and buried within the ashes of loss

we are reborn into something

far greater than we ever thought we could be.

Your heart lies

troubled and toxic

across a bridge burned

by the matches in your pocket.

Your eyes are empty vessels,

pools of captivity

holding your affection prisoner

twin strangers staring back at me.

Like a ghost

he lingered

haunting her memory,

a fallen victim

to dark sentiment

and black jealousy.

As the summer grew thin

and the leaves began to rust

she felt him fade

fade away

into the background

of her thoughts.

To her,

he was music

a symphony

awakening her senses,

an endless lullaby

orchestrated by love.

To him,

she was a puzzle

with jagged edges

he couldn't quite piece together

nor understand.

She fell in love

with the dancing butterflies

he evoked

so effortlessly,

ignoring

the taste of ash

in his kiss

and the silence

on the other end of the phone.

His youth

bled her love dry,

for the least he ever gave her

was the most she had ever known.

Tweaked to perfection

is the magnitude of your indecision

pretty words bared insignificant

by the hollow strength of your actions.

And yet,

this foolish heart bleeds with romanticized

remembrance

mourning the threadbare fabrication of your

emotions.

You say the extremes

are what capture our attention

and trigger human interest

separating the mundane

from the extraordinary.

Your potential is lost on me

because in the spectrum

of all that is sublime and ordinary

you are a disappointment.

His words left,

a bitter taste in her mouth

tainting her palette

with afterthoughts

that coated her tongue

like black coffee.

She tried and tried

to win his affection

'twas all in vain

for his love was tangled

in the throes of caffeine

and addiction.

Skin deep

They admired her painted beauty
where each expression
was a loving stroke
by a seasoned hand.

Only his eyes
looked past
symmetry and skin
tracing
the cracks underneath
and saw her painted beauty
unforgivably bland.

The Perils of Romance

She was unsure

if she idealized his character,

meticulously selecting elements

she wanted to see,

casting a blind eye

when one by one

he shed his layers

revealing who he was underneath.

It was easier to contend with her thoughts

than the reality of the situation,

and when it was all over

she wasn't sure

if who she loved was him

or her romanticized vision.

He fed her words

so delectable

and sweet

enticing her

delighting her

until

she saw his words

for what they were;

simple letters

strung together

without the depth

of love or imagination,

grand prose

without poetic truth.

Ash

She tried to ignore

the taste of ash in his kiss

and the grey pillows of smoke

that surrounded him.

While he surrendered with relief

to the temporary salvation

of smoke and drink

and left her

to contemplate their differences

in neglected isolation.

In time

she slowly felt herself falling deeper,

too deep to start anew,

her lungs filled with smoke

and her kisses

tasted like ash too.

Sacred

You are a symphony
to my senses
each breath
a sacrament.

Blessed or cursed
I know not yet
waiting for the revelation
of your inscrutable intentions.

In the light of day
her mind renounced
his beloved name.

Scrubbing
the chambers of her mind
where each letter
was lovingly engraved.

Her precious memories
remained scrupulously repressed
and she forced herself to continue
to breathe, to exist
whilst her heart beat wildly in protest.

I teach myself how to live

as the days grow crimson

bleeding into one another

each the same as before.

And Patience is not my friend

nor a virtue I claim to possess

but to survive the crimson days

Patience is a card I play close to my chest.

Resistance

She envied his casual ability
to numb himself with distractions aplenty,
while she remained stagnant
drenched in distracted thoughts
that took a wrong turn for misery.
His words
showed her who he wished to be,
with a potential that blazed brighter
than Icarus's sun.
Maybe it was a case of bloodlines
an inherited scarlet letter
from generations stained before
that caused his resolve to come undone.
The difference lay between
how he lived and what he said
tormenting her until resistance
unraveled in blue ribbons
at the edge of his bed.

What a Pity

Break the ice,

you look back at me with stranger's eyes

your face I do not recognize.

The days are for writing

the nights are for sighing

and thoughts of you stray in between.

Excuse me,

over my tongue I have no control

this poem is my confessional

your dreams I keep

your words I eat

I am starved for affection in between.

This is the end my love.

Goodbye.

Goodbye.

Wickham

Deeper than bones
the poison had spread
all consuming
until there was nothing
human left.
The thick fog had set in
the sinister deed was done
he lost his humanity that day
in his desperation to become no one.

Burdened by the troubles

of their weary souls

they followed the river

to the edge of the ocean

to escape the claustrophobia

of their skin

and their bones.

Verona

How bittersweet

when joy and sorrow mix

star crossed lovers

from the houses of Montague and Capulet.

The exchange of vows

in the dead of night

romance under the stars

tainted with bloodshed and strife.

A desperate plan

gone fatally awry

swift death comes

to the sleeping bride.

Forever burned in sonnet and memory

Juliet and her Romeo

under the moonlit balcony.

Florence

On the cobbled streets
the poet writes
black ink scratching paper
deep into the restless night.

While the dreamers dream
and the city sleeps
the poet hunts
for sufficient words
to maintain the frayed threads of her sanity
and keep her soul's peace.

Mateus

The sheltered darkness
was her secret sanctuary
amongst modern temples
in the ancient streets.

She finally understood
why the drunks and dreamers
came out at night,
for she had succumbed to both
in the space of a week.

Amsterdam

17th century canals
winding through a city
brimming with life,
where sweet Escape
lurks behind every corner
offered at a humble price.

Lakehouse

At the mercy
of her chipped lighter
and translucent white paper
to take them away
ever so briefly.

The lake a witness
to the desensitization
of lost summer innocence,
where through the trees
echoed the wail of sirens
and the bright laughter
of carefree children.

A trip to the stars
stolen moments in lost galaxies
priceless in worth,
until they returned
with the cry of a lone swan
safely back to earth.

Why is loss inevitable

why do we choose to attach our souls

to those who do not

have the stamina to stay

why is the ruin of heart break

worth precarious moments

of temporary happiness

is it merely a crafted distraction

while our bones crumble

and our hearts decay

Imprints

Poetry flowed through her veins
every rhyme imprinted on her skin,
it made her feel alive
to indulge in the love of those
who submitted themselves wholly
to human sensation.

It didn't occur to her
she never had the chance to win,
because no two hearts beat the same
and hers was lost
to the perils of fictional ruin.

Being with him
felt like
the calm before the storm.

Her heart swung back and forth
between heavy contemplation
and feather light banter.

Perhaps she would be safer
on her own.

For he was both
storm and shelter.

Gutter flower

Your taste

runs parallel to my own

for you indulge

in escaping a world

that clashes with your idealistic vision,

while I find dignified beauty

that gives birth

to struggling flowers

in every cracked pavement.

Perjury

The one who drew inspiration to her pen
could not fulfill the desires of her heart,
a summer muse he remained
locked forever in poetry and art.
She craved him
with the rage of an addict,
bargaining everything she could
for one more touch of his skin
one sacred breath of his kiss
His actions were at a discrepancy
to the words he presented,
evidence her mind contended with
but her heart refused to acknowledge.
She reached her final verdict
as both judge and jury,
drawing her final conclusion
like a circle of protection,
trapped inside another layer
of loneliness and isolation.

Naught hath wronged me
but my own hands
leading towards the destruction
they warned me against.

Blindly I turn to you
in the search for mortal redemption
while my soul flames and burns
at your expense.

Fickle hearts

Through the bright smiles
there lingers the gnawing fear
that history is repeating itself once more.

Familiar doubts creep in
and the same conversations settle
into tortuous silence.

Your eyes slide away from me
to her,
and I know
I should know better.

Because if men's hearts are fickle
why should yours be any different?

Him and Her

His grey thoughts
never drifted towards her,
while hers
were saturated with the colours of his smile.

She memorized the way the sunlight
danced across his face
and the thousand hues
burning bright in his golden eyes.

If she only knew
he only saw her as ordinary,
while her pen sought to capture him
in prose and poetry.

The Extremes

All I know are extremes
black and white,
love and hate,
the salt of tears and aches of laughter,
yearning for
the shades of grey that make it bearable.

Perhaps little glimmers of happiness
are all we can hope for
in our daily toil,
learning the truth all too late
when we shuffle off our mortal coil.

They told her

not to be so surprised

when her skin burned

and her heart erupted in flames

for what did she expect

when she danced with the devil

in playgrounds of fire

cast aplenty on earthly plains.

He wreaked havoc

on her thoughts,

a plight

on her sensibilities,

and chaos

in her heart.

When his shadow retreated

and his voice simmered to a whisper

did she come to realize,

pastures are greener

where there is peace of mind.

Shallow Waters

She wondered
if he had the depth
to love her
whole heartedly
the way she needed him to.

Or would he drown
in shallow waters
like the unfortunate one before.

For he was a drug
that she abused in abundance
and a fatal overdose
was far more preferable
than letting him go.

This is the abyss
and we're slipping over the edge
where a single word
can shatter
or save us.

This is the fall they promised
when we believed
that love alone would be enough.

This is the ending
we have the power to rewrite
if you would only try.

This is the part
where I don't know
how to make you hold on
when your eyes
slowly coax me to let go.

You have faded

like a dream

that one strives to capture in the morning

only to find empty hands

as it slips quietly away

across my pillow

through the open window

down the street

where innocent children once played.

Illusions

To endure a life
of a simple mundane existence
is both a blessing and a curse.

To live in servitude
and little consequence
diminishes our right to self-actualization
as we lose ourselves in a life of quiet worth.

In an age of false gods
we breathe in the promise of illusions
yearning to be a part of something more
that Time washed away with our youth.

Dirt and Dreams

Trying to make ends meet
the rope unwinds as the day goes by,
midnight showers bleed knee deep
chaos flickers in the morning sky.
Perhaps we are mere mortals
shuffling blind in this wayward life.
for there is madness
and peace in the unknown,
but uncertainty cuts deep,
a self-inflicted vice.
Nothing is left
but firelight
and the specter
of what once was
a dystopian world bereft
of human contact.
The end grows nigh
my skin begins to tear at the seams,
flesh and bone begging for release
in this unholy space
between dirt and dreams.

A Song in the Distance

There is a song in the distance.

Is that salvation?

For my ears are deaf to the cries of the old,

the weak,

the stricken,

the poor,

All I hear is the breaking of my own heart,

because I am selfish,

and young,

and naïve,

tried only by the whims of my own feelings,

foolishly at war with a world that has crumbled

to dust at my feet.

What was once

is now no more.

And yet there are fragments of beauty

in what I see.

Glory on earth and in the seven skies

perhaps there is hope and redemption

through a sacred life.

But right now there is nothing,

nothing

but broken words

and empty feeling.

Desperate Times

These are desperate times, my friend,

the sky is alight with fire.

Salt tears in dirty handkerchiefs seep,

the young, the old,

the sick, the grey,

how they weep.

Brace thyself, the end is near

and circumstances are dire.

There is madness in the air tonight, my friend,

see how the smoke has begun to curl.

Demon shapes in flames unfurl

hailing a warrior's cry on earth's final battlefield.

Mother Nature has turned on us, my friend,

the rite of passage no longer that of man's.

The paper sun withers as the clouds fall through

while the cult of the ordinary,

the poor, the mundane,

the depressed,

violate the Father's Law.

Be silent.

Be still.

In the wake of madness

lurk night terrors after our reckless hearts.

These are dark times, my friend,

when reflection is our own worst enemy.

I've lost myself countless times now

in mended glass,

seven years of hollow victory.

The winds chime through stained windows

the view has changed much over the years, my

friend,

no one is as they were before.

The Holy Ghost has long departed, my friend,

he left the station at 4,

with stars in his eyes and a map in his hand,

salvation walking out the front door.

This is the threshold of life and death, my friend,

I'll hold you,

to me, hold on.

The siren song sings us to sweet disaster,

as the rolling tide moves us all along.

The Gods of War are upon us, my friend,

they have sounded the trumpet of battle.

Say a prayer

for we make history tonight

inscribed in memory, forever in rhyme,

we are drowning, my friend,

drowning in these dark and desperate times.

I thought I knew

but I know not

but as I continue to learn

I realize

Man is inconsequential

and we are bound for a greater destiny

than the one they deny.

For I cannot live in a world

where concrete children

grow through the forgotten cracks

our humanity has left behind.

Is nature not the healing balm for the afflicted?

The prickle of grass underneath one's feet,

the cool whisper of the wind

through unkempt hair,

Mother Nature

breathes life anew

when we grow weary

of our concrete jungles,

and plastic screens,

drenched in troubles of our own making.

Burial rites

Bury me beneath
the quiet solitude
of this weeping willow
in an unmarked grave,
where life and death entwine
beckoning eternal rest
under the peaceful sway
of shadow and shade.

Sanctuary

Scratched and scarred
by the jagged hollows
where emerald branches
fall with easy grace
above layers of decayed leaves
and broken twigs,
life breathes anew
in the last light of summer
and brief pockets of solitude.

Afterlife

When the Angel of Death descends
and the whisper of thy soul
escapes parched lips.

When they place soft white shrouds
over thine eyes
and lower thy body
into six feet of dirt.

We shall not weep
as you are not gone
beloved one,
for you are the tree
that grows above the earth.

Mercy

If these be the renowned gates of Paradise
I beg Thy appointed guardians
not to lock Thy humble servant out
nor turn my broken feet away.

There is Hell on earth
I come to seek shelter from the world of the living,
to rest in Thy shadow is far more preferable
than to try and fail another day.

Existence has become a daily trial
I fear You forget I am only human
desperate to make sense of the madness and decay,
upon my soul You have placed too heavy a burden,
I beg for Thy mercy to release me now
or from Thy guidance witness my fall from grace.

Name

Liberate me

from my name,

for it is a burden in these treacherous times,

where people are labelled,

boxed in by the small minded

the weak,

the tyrants,

and the nervous.

Why do you not

go further than what your eyes perceive

and wonder at the magnificence

of the human soul

instead of the colour of my skin

and the ethnicity of my name.

The New Normal

Our new normal is
a world of destruction
where everyday
is a hashtag of loss.

And our new normal
is a fleeting sense of moral outrage
followed by slow desensitization
as dust settles back on our daily routine.

Our new normal
relies on the fact
that it's happening,
it's just not happening here.

Our new normal
is never going to change
until we realize
nothing about this existence
is normal at all.

Who are the people
we are fading into,
slowly becoming
all that we thought
we would never be.

Where the highlight of the week
is coming home
only to rinse and repeat
burning the hours we go through.

Our childhood heroes fade
gathering dust in old memory,
as we trade our futures
for a life so ordinary.

Do we belong
or do we merely pretend
generating false meaning
from an exiled existence.

Blind

We continue to search for signs
that validate our existence,
believing our lives to be meaningless and ordinary
until we are given one sided rationalization.

Why are we unable to read the signs
in everyday miracles
that offer sparks of illumination,
no longer having to blindly scramble
for answers in the dark.

We are connoisseurs of instant gratification

in the race to consume

temporary distractions

in our recycled culture of

brand names and superficial love

working for a future that eludes us

as we neglect the present

upon which we become dependant

caught in the vicious cycle

of second hand dreams

at the mercy of pop culture trends

prizing manufactured moments

left to wonder why

happiness eludes us in the end.

Drifter

She packed her bag
with a small hole in the left side
to ease the burden
of her wandering feet.
No one warned her
to travel was to be insatiable,
the lust to explore
conquered only by starry-eyed greed.
Each step she took led her towards
winding streets, narrow alleyways
and seas the most perfect blue,
overpowering her senses
with the gift of new experience
as her heart grew fuller and fuller
with the enchantment of discovery.
To come home was bittersweet.
'twas a fact she already knew,
but no one warned her
the aching feeling in her bones
upon the realization
she had nothing to come home to.

Fernweh

Restless hearts

seeking to belong

to homes

beyond the horizon

where they have never met

but instinctively know

this is where they are meant to be.

La Vie En Rose

Life through the pink lenses
of Parisian champagne
bubbling with mirth
overflowing with the hope
of beautiful days to come.

Pressing a kiss on cold steel
sealing our fate on love locks,
a wishful testament to young love
resting peacefully along the Pont des Arts.

A final walk along the winding river
where copper wishes
meet the Seine's watery depths
the sky blazes a fiery pink rose
kissing us goodbye
on the reluctant eve of our final sunset.

Companion

I cannot recall

a moment without you

by my side.

Like a shadow

your presence always was

entwined with mine.

From the cusp of childhood

to every heartache and lesson

we have endured together

there is no memory

I have of you

that isn't dusted with our laughter.

For you are the heart of the funfair

and the wisdom I seek

in the darkest of days.

Fate and destiny

crafted our union from birth

in the other we found a soul mate

our eternal companions on earth.

Sleep did not come easily

and the night was both friend and foe

disrupting her dreams with remembrance,

restless she lay

unable to seek shelter from her own thoughts

a helpless victim to their merciless torment.

The 4 a.m. darkness became her refuge

as she sought the comfort of faith and her pen

within the confines of the walls in her bedroom

nevermore tormented again.

Paper

was her canvas

upon which she painted

her grief, her sorrow

her disappointment

and anguish.

Her words

flowed freely

bleeding scarlet ink

the colour of her memories.

Her thoughts

once saturated sweet

thick rivers of golden honey

turned dark with remorse

drenching her pages

with verse aplenty.

For what is there for an unknown poet to gain

neither glory, nor gold

nor reputation, nor fame,

submitting to canvas

her human experience

in the hopes of literary redemption.

The Poet

Why does the poet reopen healed wounds
to pour ink on her pages
awash with rusted memories
and the histories of an untamed heart,
where every syllable caresses
her worn aches
and deep warrior scars.
Witness the dance of her pen
in the final act between the frayed lines
of contemporary art
and slow suicide.

www.ingramcontent.com/pod-product-compliance
Lightning Source LLC
Chambersburg PA
CBHW032138040426
42449CB00005B/301